**Souper Jenny**
56 East Andrews Drive NW
Atlanta, Georgia 30305
404-237-7687
souperjennyatl.com

# Souper Jenny DOES SALADS

## ATLANTA'S SOUP DIVA SHARES HER FAVORITE SALAD RECIPES

JENNIFER LEVISON

PHOTOGRAPHY BY JOEL SILVERMAN

ADDITIONAL PHOTOS BY LYNN MASCIARELLI

Schroder Media

Schroder Media
Published by Schroder Media LLC
P.O. Box 250026
Atlanta, GA 30325-0026
www.schrodermedia.com

Cover + book design: Angela K Aquino
Copy + recipe editing: Jeannette Dickey
Production editor: Jan Butsch Schroder
Production manager: Hope Mirlis
Recipe testing: Jessica Hanners & Jennifer Levison
Photography: Joel Silverman & Lynn Masciarelli
Index: Wendy Allex

ISBN: 978-0-9762288-7-5

Printed and bound in the United States
First printing, 2012

I dedicate this book to my son, Jonah,
who daily opens my eyes and heart.
And to my family for supporting every one
of my interests right from the very beginning.

sharing the glory
of the garden...

# Contents

# A love letter to Jenny

I have written four books and hundreds of articles, but this piece has proven to be one of the most difficult. To summarize my feelings for my daughter in a few paragraphs has been a daunting task.

There are so many things I could say about my Jenny. She is the youngest of my three wonderful children and my only girl. When she was little she was my "dress-up doll," and I had such fun seeing her in her perfectly coordinated outfits with big bows on her ponytails. It wasn't long before her strong will emerged and she insisted on picking out her own clothes. We still argue sometimes about what she should wear, but she usually wins.

A few memories from the years when Jenny was growing up:

Her decision at age 12 that washing and combing her hair was a waste of time...fortunately she got over that pretty quickly.

When she made the cut for her junior high choral group, and her stepfather, Don, got out the sewing machine and made her a white skirt for her performance.

The three of us eating take-out fried chicken in bed while watching movies on TV.

Jenny at age 10 in a white chef's hat serving us an elegant dinner that she made from scratch.

The Mother's Day when she had all the waitstaff in the restaurant where she worked wear a picture of me with the salutation, "Happy Mother's Day Teddi."

Her graduation from Carnegie Mellon.

The first time I saw her incredible presence onstage.

Shopping for her wedding gown.

The day she was married.

The first time I saw Jonah in her arms.

I could reminisce for many more pages, but that is not what this love letter is all about. It is about the woman that my baby girl has become. She's an inspiration to everyone who knows her, and if she wasn't my daughter, I'd want her for a good friend. Fortunately for me she is both.

"Impossible" is not a word in Jenny's vocabulary. If she wants something to happen, she will somehow make it work, and that includes finishing a triathlon this past year. Jenny puts all of herself into everything she does, and she is an expert multi-tasker. Her spirit, warmth, and charisma create the ambiance that makes Souper Jenny and Cafe Jonah places where so many people like to hang out.

Jenny was a well-trained actor and singer before she became a soup diva, and she still participates in local theater with the same drive and enthusiasm with which she does everything else. She rarely says no when asked to contribute time or food to a charity event, and her staff and friends can always count on her for a sympathetic ear and a helping hand. I will never understand how she finds the time and energy to do all that she does.

As you may have guessed, in my eyes Jenny is a superstar. She has so many reasons to be proud of herself, but if you asked her what she considers her proudest accomplishment, she would likely answer, "being Jonah's mother." She approaches motherhood like everything else,

giving it her all...and seeing her little boy's eyes light up when he sees his mommy, it's clear that her devotion has paid off.

I haven't said much about Jenny's magic touch as an entrepreneur, her skills as a hostess, or her reputation as a famous soup guru, because that's not what she is about to me. The essence of Jenny is her determination to live life to its fullest, her dedication to always seek another challenge, her willingness to take risks, her natural instincts for spreading warmth and love, and her everlasting belief that the glass is always half full.

I have had my share of career success and good fortune throughout my life. Now my claim to fame is being "Souper Jenny's Mom"...and that's just fine with me.

*Teddi Sanford*
a.k.a.
*Souper Jenny's Mom*

# Jenny's ode to Jessica

Any chef, restaurateur, or head of an organization knows there is no way to succeed as a great leader and employer without learning to delegate responsibility. This had been one of my greatest lessons in life and it's why in 2010, I finally listened to some wise folks and took the step of hiring a real, live chef.

Let me say, this was a scary proposition. Hire someone more talented than me? That would be embarrassing! Give someone complete control over the kitchen I have run for ten years and let them take on everything from making menus and dealing with kitchen staff to ordering all the food and making it look from the outside that "Jenny" is still in the building? That's a tall order.

Let me introduce you to Jessica Hanners. You may recognize her from our first cookbook when she was still a server at Souper Jenny. Jessica left the front staff in 2007 to go to culinary school, but from the very beginning I always admired her take on food and freshness. She knew what kind of food I was producing, and she understood the importance of a top notch kitchen that puts love and respect into its work. This has always been my priority when cooking and creating and it's refreshing to watch someone else put that same love and attention into her daily work.

I'm pretty sure, no in fact I am positive, that I drove Jessica nuts for a good six months. I constantly lurked around the kitchen pretending I was just visiting and making slight suggestions. "Doesn't that need more color?" "Have you really added the cheese yet? Hmm. Looks different." Jessica was a trooper and answered each question kindly and took each suggestion with grace.

I realized months later that in order for someone to fly with your vision, you must give her the room to do it, so I gradually backed out of the daily routine and gave Jess the space to do her job. I realize now that it isn't the actual cooking that I miss, but the daily ritual of being there with my co-workers and creating a menu together. I miss hearing about Irene's kids and Leticia's new baby, so I have created a new ritual of coming by daily and visiting instead of looking over everyone's shoulder. I get to see firsthand how Jessica leads her team and I recognize daily that I made the right choice.

I tell you all this so you know that no one succeeds alone. It truly takes a village to operate even the tiniest cafe, and I wouldn't have been able to take on a second restaurant and a second cookbook, not to mention parenting a terrific eight-year-old, without a lot of help. This past year has been filled with many transitions and I could not have made them smoothly without giving up some control, which is never easy to do!

Thank you Jessica for taking over the kitchen at Souper Jenny without compromising my vision. I see it in your work every day and it is appreciated from the bottom of my heart.

Jenny

...it's all in a day's work for jessica!

AS I SIT DOWN TO WRITE THE INTRODUCTION FOR OUR SECOND COOKBOOK, I AM LITERALLY LAUGHING OUT LOUD BECAUSE I NEVER IMAGINED IN A MILLION YEARS THAT THERE WOULD BE A SECOND COOKBOOK! THE INSPIRATION FOR *SOUPER JENNY COOKS* CAME FROM MY FRIEND HOPE, WHO INFORMED ME THAT AFTER TEN YEARS IT WAS TIME TO PUT MY RECIPES DOWN ON PAPER. I GRUDGINGLY AGREED, BUT AS THE BOOK BEGAN TO TAKE SHAPE, I FELL IN LOVE WITH THE COLLABORATION AMONG THE PHOTOGRAPHER, DESIGNER, MYSELF, AND EVERYONE INVOLVED RIGHT DOWN TO THE LAST RECIPE TESTER. I LOVED SEEING PHOTOS OF MY FAMILY AND STAFF SCATTERED IN WITH THE RECIPES, AND IT MADE ME INCREDIBLY GRATEFUL TO SEE HOW HAPPY AND FULL MY LIFE REALLY IS.

Everyone in my community knows that Souper Jenny serves delicious, healthy and hearty soups, but as the years progressed, our kitchen is also loved for its incredible salads. So I decided that sharing some of our favorite, easy salad recipes in a second book would make a natural companion for our soup book.

I am a salad fanatic and am constantly on the prowl for the perfect combinations to offer my friends, family and guests of our restaurants.

Yes. Restaurants, plural. Since our first cookbook we have opened a second cafe right around the corner from Souper Jenny. Named after my son, Jonah, Cafe Jonah and the Magical Attic is my ode to healthy, fabulous food with a bit of my metaphysical side thrown in. Downstairs the cozy cafe offers fabulous coffees and heart healthy breakfast options, and then transitions to a high-end lunch salad bar where raw kale salad with local apples and maple dressing sits alongside organic chicken salad with yogurt dressing, and many more options. The upstairs is a haven for those wishing to find a quiet place to chat, browse through a collection of my favorite spiritual books and gifts, or indulge in a psychic reading or session with a healer.

Cafe Jonah has been a great testing ground for the salads in this book. I like to be onsite myself to ask guests for their feedback on a certain dressing or spice, and believe me, I've heard some VERY honest feedback!

A couple of thoughts to keep in mind as you read through this book. First of all, I pride myself on super easy, non-complicated recipes that even the most novice salad maker

can master. My favorite meals consist of fresh, high-quality ingredients put together in a simple way. There is nothing better than a perfectly sun-ripened tomato dressed with a splash of fruity vinegar, a specialty oil, and a touch of salt and pepper. What more is there?

Next, please experiment! There are no laws for creating your perfect salad, so live it up and try your own combinations. Don't like almonds? Try replacing them or omitting them altogether. I like almonds for their crunch. But find your own favorites and just use this book as a guide to get you started.

Last, but not least, I beg you to buy local when you can. Your farmers' markets are meccas for the best produce you'll ever eat, and what could be better than meeting the farmers who grew those gorgeous bunches of carrots and dinosaur kale? Often people don't understand why produce grown nearby can be a bit more expensive, but think about what is involved. Local farmers aren't growing thousands and thousands of pounds of pesticide-laden produce and shipping it thousands of miles so it can ripen in your neighborhood grocery store. When I buy lettuce at my market, I know it was picked nearby the night before by the very farmer who brought it. In my opinion, there is no comparison.

Okay, enough preaching. I hope you use this book to get your creative juices flowing. If you are not totally inspired, pour yourself a big glass of wine and enjoy the pictures of my family!

Remember, I am always available for feedback. Feel free to stop by one of the restaurants. If you're not in Atlanta, email me at souperjenny@aol.com.

Where
we are
today...

the garden is
nature's best classroom!

# Vegetarian Salads

Simple French Salad

Roasted Greek Style Vegetable Salad with Garlic Chips & Feta

Fattoush, My Way!

Fresh Green Beans with Homemade Walnut Pesto

Super Greens

Raw Vegetable Slaw

Fennel Apple Slaw

Roasted Fresh Figs with Bleu Cheese & Honey on a Bed of Baby Arugula

Black Bean, Corn, Avocado & Red Onion Salad with Cilantro Vinaigrette

Baby Spinach, Red Pears, Bleu Cheese & Toasted Hazelnuts with Sage & Honey Vinaigrette

Roasted Butternut Squash, Baby Spinach & Bleu Cheese with Maple Ginger Vinaigrette

Roasted Delicata Squash Salad with Wilted Greens & Pumpkin Seeds

Jessica's Raw Brussels Sprouts & Kale Salad

Jenny's Artichoke & Favorite Dip

Rosemary Scented Lentil Salad with Apricot, Feta & Mint

Spaghetti Squash Salad Two Ways

Jenny's Capotouille

Wild Mushroom Salad with Shaved Manchego over Baby Arugula

Roasted Cauliflower Salad with Dates & Golden Raisins

Roasted Beet Salad with Goat Cheese & Fresh Orange Salsa

Pan-Grilled Asparagus

Autumn Slaw with Macadamia Nuts & Maple Ginger Dressing

Ode to Heidi Swanson Roasted Chickpea & Kale Salad

Baby Spinach, Pomegranate Seeds, Feta, Toasted Pine Nuts & Pomegranate-Shallot Dressing

# Simple French Salad

**SERVES: 4 TO 6**

For the dressing:
1 shallot
1 tablespoon smooth Dijon mustard
2 teaspoons fresh tarragon
1/4 cup white wine vinegar
1 cup extra virgin olive oil
salt and pepper

For the salad:
12 cups lettuce of choice (I like Belgian endive or butter lettuce)
1 cup chopped, mixed fresh herbs (I use flat leaf parsley, chives,
  chervil and cilantro)

In a food processor, puree shallot, mustard, tarragon, and vinegar. While machine is running, slowly drizzle in olive oil. Add salt and pepper to taste.

Mix greens and herbs and add dressing to coat lightly. Remaining dressing will last up to a week refrigerated.

Long ago, I was married to a Frenchman... but that's another book! Anyway, I loved nothing more than this simple salad his mother made when we visited his family in the southwest of France. So simple, yet delicious!

simplicity at its finest...

# Roasted Greek Style Vegetable Salad
## with Garlic Chips & Feta

**SERVES: 8**

This salad is a favorite to get a lot of vegetables into my diet in one meal. Roasting vegetables at high heat brings out the sweetness of each individually. For best results and desired doneness (though not essential), roast each vegetable separately on individual sheet pans. Good hot or cold.

2 medium yellow squash, quartered vertically
2 medium zucchini, quartered vertically
1 pound bunch asparagus, bottom 2 inches of stalks removed
2 large portobello mushrooms, cut into 1/2 inch wide pieces
2 medium red onions, cut into rings
1 each red, yellow, green and orange pepper, seeds removed, cut into thick, long strips
extra virgin olive oil
1 tablespoon chopped fresh rosemary
1 tablespoon chopped fresh oregano
salt and pepper to taste
2 lemons, juiced
8 ounces crumbled feta
6 large cloves garlic, peeled

Heat oven to 400°. Toss each vegetable with a little olive oil (about 2 teaspoons) and sprinkle chopped rosemary on half and chopped oregano on other half. Roast to desired doneness, about 15-20 minutes, turning halfway through cooking time. A slightly charred or caramelized look will give you the best flavors. Once vegetables are roasted, put all in a mixing bowl and toss with lemon juice, salt and pepper to taste. Arrange vegetables on a plate, topping with crumbled feta and garlic chips.

Garlic Chips:
Thinly slice garlic cloves and place in small saute pan with 1 inch olive oil to cover. Turn heat on medium to low flame and cook garlic just until golden brown. Remove with a slotted spoon to drain on paper towels.

# Fattoush, My Way!

**SERVES: 6 TO 8**

3 pieces pita bread
2 tablespoons extra virgin olive oil
salt and pepper
garlic powder
4 handfuls baby spinach
2 cups chickpeas, cooked
2 cups halved cherry tomatoes (preferably multi-colored)
1 cup kalamata olives, pitted and chopped
1/2 cup chopped fresh mint leaves
1/2 cup chopped flat leaf parsley
1 European cucumber, sliced lengthwise, then cut into half moons
1 cup Cafe Jonah's Fresh Lemon Dressing (see page 100)

Preheat oven to 350°. Cut pita into triangles; each piece should yield 8 triangles. In a bowl, toss pita with oil, salt, pepper, and garlic powder to taste. Bake 15 minutes or until golden brown. Let cool.

In a large mixing bowl, toss together all vegetables and herbs. Break cooled pita chips into smaller pieces and add to salad. Add dressing sparingly and toss until everything is evenly coated.

I love Lebanese food and fattoush is one of my "go to" salads for entertaining since it's something different for most guests. Try this for your next get-together and relish all the "oohs" & "aahs"!

# Fresh Green Beans with Homemade Walnut Pesto

**SERVES: 6 TO 8**

1 1/2 pounds fresh green beans, trimmed
1/2 cup chopped walnuts
1/2 cup basil leaves
1/2 cup shredded aged Parmesan
2 cloves garlic, peeled
1 tablespoon fresh lemon juice
1 cup extra virgin olive oil
salt and pepper

For the beans:
Bring a large pot of heavily salted water to a boil, add beans to pot and blanch for 2 minutes. While beans are blanching, prepare a large bowl of ice water. Drain beans and immediately submerge them in ice water for a few minutes to stop cooking and set bright green color. Remove beans from water and dry on paper towels.

For the walnut pesto:
In a food processor, puree walnuts, basil, Parmesan, garlic, and lemon juice. With machine running, add olive oil slowly.

Toss beans with pesto and season to taste with salt and pepper.

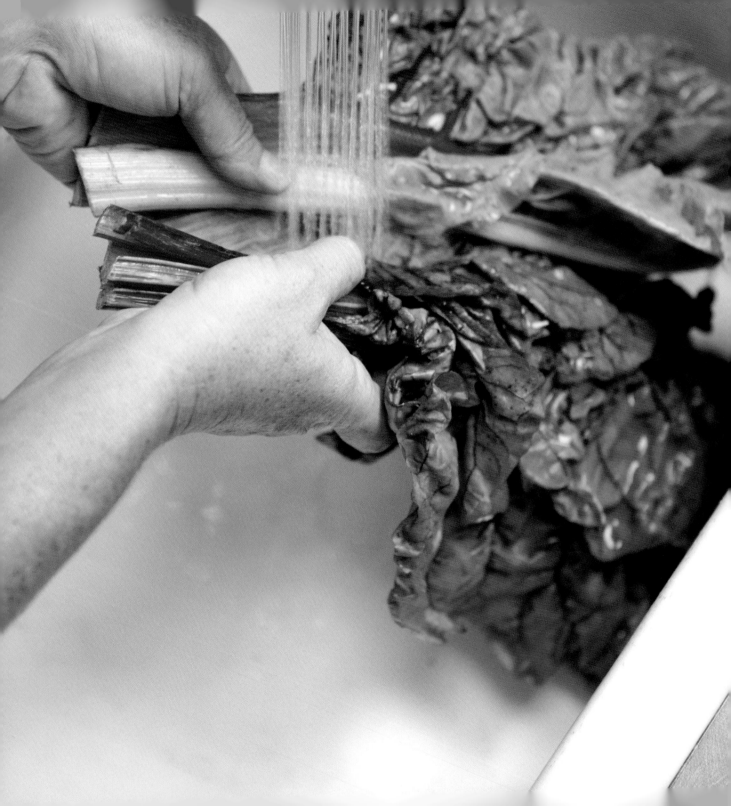

# Super Greens

**SERVES: 6**

If you ever wanted to know how to keep your green vegetables a beautiful bright green color, follow this easy recipe and you will wow your guests and yourself! This is delicious hot or cold.

1 bunch of kale, Lacinato if available, ribs removed
1 bunch asparagus, 2 inches cut from bottoms of stalks
1 pound green beans, trimmed
1 bunch Swiss chard, ribs removed
1 tablespoon extra virgin olive oil
1 tablespoon favorite fruit flavored vinegar
1 tablespoon fresh lemon zest
salt and pepper

Bring a medium soup pot of heavily salted water to a boil. Prepare a big bowl of ice water. Blanch vegetables one at a time for 1 1/2 minutes and plunge into ice water to stop cooking and set color, keeping water cold for each vegetable. Drain and thoroughly pat dry vegetables as cooled. Transfer to a mixing bowl and toss with olive oil, vinegar, lemon zest, salt and pepper to taste. Can be served any temperature.

# Raw Vegetable Slaw

**SERVES: 8**

1 yellow pepper, julienned
1 red pepper, julienned
1 orange pepper, julienned
1 green pepper, julienned
4 cups broccoli slaw
2 cups Napa cabbage, thinly sliced
2 cups fresh baby spinach, chopped or cut into strips
2 garlic cloves, minced
1/2 cup chopped fresh dill
1 small jalapeno, seeded and chopped
1/4 cup apple cider vinegar
1 cup extra virgin olive oil
salt and pepper

Put all prepared vegetables in a bowl and toss with some salt and pepper.

Dressing: Put garlic, dill, jalapeno, and vinegar in bowl and stir to combine. Slowly whisk in oil until all emulsified. Salt and pepper to taste and dress slaw with desired amount.

"Julienne" means to cut into thin, uniform strips. Some like to use a mandoline, which can offer a perfect julienne. But good knife skills can work just as well.

IF YOU'RE
HAPPY
AND YOU
KNOW IT
CLAP YOUR
HANDS

my friend, ethan,
came to visit the
souper jenny food truck!

# Fennel Apple Slaw

**SERVES: 4 TO 6**

2 tablespoons minced shallot
1 tablespoon white wine vinegar
salt and pepper
2 tablespoons extra virgin olive oil
3 heads Belgian endive, halved lengthwise, cored and thinly sliced crosswise
3 small fennel bulbs, halved lengthwise, cored and thinly sliced crosswise
1 large Fuji or other crisp apple, halved lengthwise, cored and thinly sliced

Whisk together the shallot, vinegar, salt and pepper to taste in a non-reactive bowl. Add olive oil slowly, whisking to fully emulsify. Add endive, fennel, and apple to dressing and toss to coat.

What is non-reactive?
Material that won't react
chemically with your food.
For bowls, use stainless steel,
glass or plastic.

# Roasted Fresh Figs with Bleu Cheese & Honey
## on a Bed of Baby Arugula

**SERVES: 6**

18 fresh figs, split lengthwise, stems removed
1 tablespoon olive oil, plus 2 tablespoons
6 ounces best honey available
18 ounces baby arugula
8 ounces your favorite bleu cheese
1 cup toasted pecans
zest of 1 lemon
2 tablespoons fig balsamic vinegar or any fruit vinegar
salt and pepper

Preheat oven to 400°. Place figs on a sheet pan, flesh side up, and brush with 1 tablespoon olive oil. Roast for 15 to 20 minutes. After removing from oven, drizzle honey over figs. Lay arugula on plates. Top with 6 fig halves. Sprinkle bleu cheese, toasted pecans, then lemon zest over. Drizzle on vinegar and 2 tablespoons olive oil, salt and pepper to taste.

# Black Bean, Corn, Avocado & Red Onion Salad
## with Cilantro Vinaigrette

**SERVES: 6**

3 cups dried black beans, soaked overnight
2 bunches cilantro, stems removed
2 cloves garlic, peeled
1/4 cup fresh lemon juice
1 cup extra virgin olive oil
salt and pepper
4 ears corn, kernels cut from cob
1 large red pepper, diced small
2 ripe avocados, pitted and diced
1 small red onion, diced small

Soak black beans overnight according to package instructions. In a stock pot, bring beans, 1 teaspoon salt, and 10 cups water to a rolling boil. Lower heat and simmer beans about 45 minutes, until tender. Drain.

In a food processor, puree cilantro, garlic, and lemon juice. While machine is running, slowly add oil. Salt and pepper to taste.

In a bowl, mix beans, corn, red pepper, avocado, and red onion. Dress salad to your personal taste.

How to perfectly prep an avocado:

# Baby Spinach, Red Pears, Bleu Cheese & Toasted Hazelnuts
## with Sage & Honey Vinaigrette

**SERVES: 6**

For the vinaigrette:
6 tablespoons white balsamic vinegar
1/2 shallot, peeled
2 teaspoons chopped fresh sage
2 tablespoons honey
2 teaspoons smooth Dijon mustard
salt and pepper
1/2 cup extra virgin olive oil

In a small blender or food processor, blend all except the oil. Drizzle in oil slowly with machine running.

For the salad:
6 cups baby spinach
3 ripe pears, halved, cored, each half sliced into 8 thin pieces
2 cups crumbled bleu cheese (or substitute feta, goat cheese, or shredded smoked Gouda)
1 cup toasted hazelnuts, roughly chopped

I like to compose this salad on individual plates. First place a cup of spinach on each plate. Then scatter about 1/2 a pear on top of spinach, crumble cheese on top of pear, and finally sprinkle nuts on top of cheese. Drizzle dressing over each salad.

# Roasted Butternut Squash, Baby Spinach & Bleu Cheese
## with Maple Ginger Vinaigrette

**SERVES: 6**

3 cups butternut squash, peeled and cubed
2 tablespoons extra virgin olive oil, plus 1 cup for dressing
1 cup toasted pine nuts (toasted in 350° oven, 15 minutes)
2 fingers ginger, peeled and grated
1 tablespoon fresh lemon juice
1/4 cup apple cider vinegar
1 cup maple syrup
salt and pepper
12 cups fresh baby spinach
2 cups crumbled bleu cheese

Preheat oven to 450°. Toss butternut squash with 2 tablespoons olive oil. Spread on a baking sheet and roast for 30 to 40 minutes, turning several times, until cooked through and lightly browned. Cool to room temperature.

Prepare dressing while squash is roasting. In a food processor, puree together ginger, lemon juice, and vinegar. Add maple syrup and while machine is running, slowly drizzle in remaining cup of olive oil. Salt and pepper to taste.

In a large bowl, toss spinach with butternut squash, bleu cheese, pine nuts. Add dressing to coat.

This is an easy salad that looks fancy and is perfect for the holidays. You can now find fresh butternut squash peeled and cubed in most grocery stores.

When I say a "finger" I mean to literally look at your index finger and choose a size that just about matches its length and width.
All fingers are different... It will be close enough!

lunch time at cafe jonah...

# Roasted Delicata Squash Salad
## with Wilted Greens & Pumpkin Seeds

**SERVES: 4 TO 6**

Delicata squash is one of the only winter varieties that does not need peeling. When cooked, the skin is delicate and beautiful.

2 small delicata squash, cut in half lengthwise, seeds removed,
   sliced into half moons
3 tablespoons extra virgin olive oil
1 tablespoon maple syrup
2 big handfuls baby spinach
2 big handfuls Swiss chard, ribs removed, leaves julienned
2 big handfuls kale, ribs removed, julienned
2 bunches escarole, chopped
1 cup toasted pumpkin seeds
3 tablespoons fruit vinegar, your choice
salt and pepper

Heat oven to 400°. Toss delicata squash with 2 tablespoons olive oil and maple syrup. Lightly salt and pepper, transfer to sheet pan in a single layer, and roast for 15 to 20 minutes. Let cool.

In a saute pan, heat remaining 1 tablespoon olive oil. Saute greens one at a time until wilted, adding a little more oil if needed. Remove to a large bowl once wilted. Mix all greens together and salt and pepper to taste.

Lay greens on a platter. Scatter squash over greens and sprinkle toasted pumpkin seeds on top. Drizzle vinegar over the dish, and voila! Delicious any temperature.

# Jessica's Raw Brussels Sprouts & Kale Salad

**SERVES: 4 TO 6**

1/2 cup coarsely chopped almonds
2 bunches Tuscan kale, center stems removed, julienned
1 pound Brussels sprouts, trimmed and thinly sliced
1 cup grated Parmesan or Asiago cheese
1 cup Cafe Jonah's Fresh Lemon Dressing (page 100)

Preheat oven to 350°. Toast chopped almonds for about 10 to 15 minutes until golden brown. Set aside and cool.

In a large mixing bowl, combine kale, Brussels sprouts, Parmesan and almonds. Slowly toss with dressing a little at a time until you have the desired amount.

Whenever Jessica makes this salad at Souper Jenny, people go crazy asking for the recipe and want to know when we'll have it again. This is so easy and these dark green, raw veggies are full of vitamins and antioxidents.

OUR PASSION

a fun day working the
souper jenny food truck!

# Jenny's Artichoke
## and Favorite Dip

**SERVES: 1 TO 2**

For the artichoke:
1 artichoke
1/2 cup fresh lemon juice
2 teaspoons baking soda

Wash artichoke and remove outer leaves. With knife cut stem down so artichoke can sit balanced. With scissors cut off tops of leaves to remove thorns. Dip artichoke in lemon juice to prevent discoloration.

Put 2 inches water, baking soda, and remaining lemon juice in a pot and bring to a boil. Place steamer basket with artichoke in pot. Cover and lower heat to simmer for 45 minutes. Leaves should easily pull away and knife should easily pierce through the bottom. Remove artichoke from pot and dry upside down.

Favorite Dip:
1 tablespoon Durkee's Famous Sauce
1 tablespoon Dijon mustard
1 tablespoon canola oil mayonnaise
1 teaspoon chopped chives
1 teaspoon fresh lemon juice

Mix all ingredients together, dip artichoke leaves and enjoy!

I think my favorite vegetable in the universe is the beautiful artichoke, and I miss living in L.A. where they are abundant year round. There are many ways to cook artichokes. I tested 5 different methods to discover the greenest, most tender deliciousness, and here is my winner. Multiply quantities to suit your needs.

**Equipment Note:**

Please use all stainless steel equipment when making this recipe: pot, steamer basket, scissors, and knives. Stainless steel is a non-reactive metal and allows the artichoke to retain its color as you prep and cook.

# Rosemary Scented Lentil Salad
## with Apricot, Feta & Mint

**SERVES: 4 TO 6**

Lentils star in several of my favorite side dishes and I'm always looking for new, interesting combinations. Try this Mediterranean favorite.

1 pound brown lentils, rinsed and picked through
3 sprigs rosemary
5 fresh apricots, pits removed, diced
1 cup feta cheese, crumbled
1/4 cup chopped fresh mint
1/4 cup lemon infused olive oil
2 tablespoons pomegranate molasses or apricot jam
salt and pepper

In a large pot, cover lentils with cold water; add rosemary. Bring to a boil, lower to a simmer and partially cover until lentils are cooked through but still holding their shape, about 20 minutes. Drain well, discard rosemary and transfer to a large mixing bowl.

Gently fold in apricots, feta, mint, olive oil, molasses, salt and pepper to taste.

# Spaghetti Squash Salad Two Ways

**BOTH SERVE: 6 TO 8**

Cooking the squash:
1 large spaghetti squash
2 teaspoons extra virgin olive oil
salt and pepper

Heat oven to 400°. Split spaghetti squash lengthwise and remove pulp and seeds.
Brush insides of squash with olive oil, salt and pepper. Place squash face down
on sheet pan and roast for 1 hour. Let squash cool. With a fork, gently pull out the
spaghetti squash – it will come out in strands similar to spaghetti.

## Favorite Ginger Spaghetti Squash

1 cooked spaghetti squash
2 teaspoons sesame oil
2 teaspoons canola oil
1 tablespoon tamari
1 tablespoon rice vinegar
1/4 cup candied ginger
1 bunch cilantro, stems removed,
  chopped
1/2 cup crushed roasted peanuts
  (optional)

Toss all ingredients together.

## Greek Style Spaghetti Squash

1 cooked spaghetti squash
1 tablespoon extra virgin olive oil
juice of 1 lemon
1/2 European cucumber, skin on,
  chopped in small dice
1 cup chopped Roma tomato
1 cup crumbled feta
1/2 cup kalamata olives, chopped
1 bunch flat leaf parsley, stems
  removed, chopped
1/4 cup mint leaves, chopped

Toss all ingredients together.

# Welcome to Cafe Jonah

Batdorf & Bronson Coffees          1⁹⁹
Cappuccino & Latte (double shot drinks)   3²⁵
Zen Tea    2⁵⁰

## Breakfast
- Organic Egg & Cheese Breakfast Sandwich  3⁹⁵
- Organic Egg Quiche of the Day a la carte  5⁰⁰
                                w/side  8⁹⁵
- Organic Egg Frittata  a la carte  5⁰⁰
                    w/side  8⁹⁵
- Steel Cut Oatmeal (gogi berry, flax seed, chia seed) 3⁹⁵

## Lunch
- Panini  a la carte  7⁰⁰  w/side  8⁹⁵

## Community Table (served w/ homemade flatbread or gluten free crackers)
* 1 choice   7⁰⁰
* 2 choices  13⁰⁰
* 3 choices  16⁰⁰
* oh just a bite of that! 1⁰⁰ each

## Daily Hot Special  served w/   8⁹⁵
            artisan greens

* We donate 10% of
our daily sales to
local charities year round.
Please enjoy our
COMMUNITY!

# Jenny's Capotouille

**SERVES: 6**

You're right! I couldn't decide if I liked ratatouille or caponata better, so I've combined these two favorites and I think the outcome is delicious. It's great as a salad or as a side with your favorite protein. Serve hot or at room temperature.

1 cup vegetable or canola oil
1 Vidalia or other sweet onion, chopped
4 cloves garlic, thinly sliced
1 teaspoon red chili flakes (optional)
1 red bell pepper, diced
1 yellow pepper, diced
1 yellow squash, diced
1 zucchini, diced
1 cup green beans, trimmed and halved
1/2 large eggplant, peeled and cubed (bite-size)
2 cups butternut squash, peeled and cubed
2 medium tomatoes, chopped
1 tablespoon tomato paste
1 tablespoon sugar
1 cup Greek olives, pitted
1 cup basil leaves, chopped

Heat 1/2 cup oil. Saute onions 5 minutes. Add garlic and chili flakes and saute another 2 to 3 minutes. Add peppers, yellow squash and zucchini to onions and saute 5 minutes. Add green beans and eggplant and saute another 5 minutes. Add butternut squash, tomatoes, tomato paste and sugar. Pour in enough water to cover half of vegetables. Cover and simmer 30 minutes.

Preheat oven to 400°. Lift vegetables out of liquid and spread into a roasting pan. Pour half of the liquid remaining over vegetables and roast for 30 minutes. Remove pan from oven. Toss in olives and basil and serve hot, or let cool and refrigerate overnight.

# Wild Mushroom Salad with Shaved Manchego
## over Baby Arugula

**SERVES: 6 TO 8**

For the mushrooms:
1 tablespoon extra virgin olive oil
3 sprigs rosemary
3 cloves garlic, minced
6 ounces lobster mushrooms, thinly sliced
12 ounces portobello mushrooms, sliced
5 ounces shitake mushrooms, sliced
3 ounces enoki or white beech mushrooms, ends removed
1/2 cup your favorite flavored vinegar (I love Cat Cora's vinegar
    with thyme and honey)
salt and pepper

For the salad:
12 ounces baby arugula
1 1/2 cups shaved or grated Manchego cheese
extra virgin olive oil
flavored vinegar

Heat saute pan, add oil. Add rosemary, garlic, and lobster mushrooms and saute 5 minutes. Add portobellos and saute 5 minutes more. Add shitakes and saute another 5 minutes. Finally, add enoki and cook for 2 minutes. Turn off heat and stir in vinegar and salt and pepper to taste.

To serve, divide arugula evenly among plates or lay all on a platter. Layer mushrooms on greens, top with Manchego, and drizzle a little more vinegar and olive oil over all.

I love mushrooms, particularly wild mushrooms. This is a fantastic and easy fall or winter salad. For a hot salad, I reheat the mixture before putting it on the arugula, or I ditch the greens and turn this into a fabulous side dish. Leftovers make a wonderful addition to soup.

(If you can't find lobster mushrooms, just use more portobellos or shiitakes.)

## Cleaning Mushrooms

I tend to wipe down my mushrooms with a damp cloth rather than hosing them down with water. You can also submerge more delicate mushrooms in water to shake off dirt, then lay on paper towels to dry.

# Roasted Cauliflower Salad
## with Dates & Golden Raisins

**SERVES: 4**

*I love mixing sweet and savory flavors as well as different textures, and cauliflower is one of those vegetables that just isn't used enough. This is a delicious dish that is good hot or room temperature.*

1 large head cauliflower, broken into florets
2 tablespoons extra virgin olive oil
1 tablespoon good fig or balsamic vinegar
1 cup pitted dates, sliced thin
1/2 cup golden raisins
1/2 cup chopped flat leaf parsley
salt and pepper

Heat oven to 375°. Toss cauliflower with olive oil and roast until a bit brown and crispy, about 30 minutes. Remove from oven and, still on sheet pan, drizzle vinegar on hot cauliflower. Let cool, then toss with dates, raisins, parsley, salt and pepper, and a bit more olive oil if needed.

# Roasted Beet Salad
## with Goat Cheese & Fresh Orange Salsa

**SERVES: 4 TO 6**

6 medium red or gold beets
2 tablespoons extra virgin olive oil, plus 2 tablespoons for dressing
3 oranges, peeled, sectioned, rough chopped
1/2 red onion, sliced thin
2 tablespoons rice wine vinegar
1 bunch cilantro, stemmed and chopped
6 ounces goat cheese (or bleu cheese)
salt and pepper

Preheat oven to 400°. Coat beets with 2 tablespoons olive oil, wrap in foil, and roast on a sheet pan for 2 hours, or until tender when pierced with a fork. Let beets cool a bit, then with a towel (to prevent red-dyed hands), rub gently to remove skins. Cut beets into medium bite-size pieces.

In a non-reactive bowl, toss together (by hand is best since the ingredients are fragile) beets, oranges, and onion. Add remaining oil, vinegar, cilantro and toss. Add goat cheese and gently toss again. Salt and pepper to taste.

I love roasted beets any time of the year. Roasting brings out their natural sweetness. Beets paired with creamy goat cheese and a tangy orange salsa... Yum!

this is eric — a loyal part of our team!

# Pan-Grilled Asparagus

**SERVES: 4**

I have a confession. I love grilled asparagus year round. Even when it's too cold to fire up the grill, I find that my grill pan offers excellent flavor and a quick option for one of my all-time favorite veggies.

2 bunches asparagus
2 tablespoons extra virgin olive oil scented with lemon
   or rosemary, plus a bit more
2 tablespoons capers
1 fresh lemon
salt and pepper

Bend asparagus until the tough ends snap off; discard ends. Toss asparagus in two tablespoons olive oil. Heat grill pan and place asparagus spears on hot pan (in a single layer). Cook for about eight minutes, turning often and letting it char a bit. Remove from heat and spread on a platter. Sprinkle with capers, drizzle a bit more oil over asparagus, and squeeze fresh lemon juice over. Salt and pepper to taste.

# Autumn Slaw
## with Macadamia Nuts
## & Maple Ginger Dressing

**SERVES: 4 TO 6**

1 cup macadamia nuts
2 teaspoons butter
2 tablespoons sugar
1/2 teaspoon chili flakes
1/2 red cabbage, core removed and shredded
1/2 green cabbage, core removed and shredded
2 cups shredded carrots
1 cup snow peas, trimmed and julienned
1 mango, pit removed and julienned
1/4 cup chopped fresh mint
1 cup cilantro leaves
1 1/2 cups Maple Ginger Dressing (page 101)

In a dry pan, toast macadamias for about five minutes until golden. Add butter, sugar, and chili flakes and toast another five to seven minutes. Put aside.

In a large mixing bowl, mix cabbages, carrots, snow peas, mango, mint, and cilantro. Slowly add dressing and toss until you have the desired consistency.

# Ode To Heidi Swanson
# Roasted Chickpea & Kale Salad

**SERVES: 4**

One of my favorite all natural cooks, Heidi Swanson, has been an inspiration for my vegetarian creations. Her roasted chickpeas make a fabulous snack and are even better in this simple salad.

1 1/2 cups cooked chickpeas, drained and dried
1 tablespoon extra virgin olive oil
zest of half a lemon
1/2 teaspoon chopped fresh rosemary
1/2 teaspoon chopped fresh oregano
1/4 teaspoon sea salt
3/4 teaspoon sweet paprika
3/4 teaspoon hot paprika
1 large bunch kale, stems removed, julienned.
1 pint cherry tomatoes, halved
1/2 cup golden raisins or sun-dried cherries
1 cup Cafe Jonah's Fresh Lemon Dressing (page 100)

Preheat oven to 400°. Spread chickpeas on baking sheet in a single layer and roast for 10 minutes. Stir chickpeas around and roast another 10 minutes or until golden brown and crispy. Add oil, lemon zest, rosemary, oregano, sea salt, and paprikas to pan and stir to coat chickpeas. Roast 3 minutes more. Remove from oven and cool.

In a large salad bowl, massage kale for five minutes to break down fibers. Add chickpeas, tomatoes, raisins, and dressing and toss to coat.

# Baby Spinach, Pomegranate Seeds, Feta, Toasted Pine Nuts
## With Pomegranate Shallot Dressing

**SERVES: 4 TO 6**

1/2 cup pine nuts
1/4 cup pomegranate molasses
1 1/2 tablespoons white wine vinegar
2 teaspoons minced shallots
1/4 teaspoon salt
2 tablespoons extra virgin olive oil
6 cups baby spinach
1/2 cup pomegranate seeds
1 cup crumbled feta

Heat oven to 350°. Toast pine nuts for about 10 minutes until golden brown. Whisk together molasses, vinegar, shallots, and salt. Drizzle in oil whisking vigorously to emulsify.

In a large bowl, toss together spinach, pomegranate seeds, pine nuts, and feta. Add dressing to taste and toss.

You can extract seeds by opening pomegranate (see photo) and carefully popping seeds free from the membrane. I often buy pomegranate seeds at my favorite Whole Foods!

the magic of gardening

# Four Perfect Tomato Salads

Everyone needs to know that the prime time to eat tomatoes is in the summer! Tomatoes are available year round in most cities, but there is something simply perfect about a summer grown tomato. Head to your local farmers' market and treat yourself! Here are a few of my favorite ways to serve this delectable fruit.

**Heirloom Tomato Salad with Fig Vinegar**

**Tomato Avocado Salad**

**Vine Ripe Tomato & Lump Crabmeat**

**Pan Roasted Cherry Tomatoes with Ricotta Salata**

# Heirloom Tomato Salad
## with Fig Vinegar

**SERVES: 4 TO 6**

4 heirloom or "ugly" tomatoes
fig vinegar
1/4 cup extra virgin olive oil
1/2 cup thin sliced fresh basil
sea salt and freshly ground pepper

Slice and arrange tomatoes (see picture on right)

Drizzle with fig vinegar and olive oil. Scatter basil over, and salt and pepper to taste.

# Tomato Avocado Salad

**SERVES: 4**

2 yellow tomatoes, sliced
2 red tomatoes, sliced
2 avocados, pitted and sliced
3 ounces goat cheese, crumbled
2 tablespoons chopped cilantro
1/4 cup extra virgin olive oil
1 lemon, squeezed over avocado to prevent discoloration
salt and pepper

Arrange tomatoes and avocados on a platter, alternating colors. Crumble goat cheese over and then scatter on cilantro. Drizzle olive oil over, and salt and pepper to taste.

# Vine Ripe Tomato & Lump Crabmeat

**SERVES: 4**

3 vine ripe tomatoes, different colors, sliced thin
1/2 European cucumber, sliced in rounds
16 ounces fresh lump crabmeat, picked through
1 cup Greek yogurt
1/4 cup buttermilk
juice of 1 lemon
1 tablespoon chopped fresh parsley
1 tablespoon chopped fresh dill
salt and pepper

On four plates, arrange tomatoes and cucumbers alternating in a circular pattern. Divide crabmeat into four portions and mound in the middle of each plate of tomatoes.

In a small bowl, combine yogurt, buttermilk, lemon, parsley, and dill. Salt and pepper to taste. Ladle over salad.

# Pan Roasted Cherry Tomatoes with Ricotta Salata

**SERVES: 4 TO 6**

What is ricotta salata? It is a version of ricotta that has been pressed, dried and salted. Very similar to feta cheese and is delicious!

2 tablespoons extra virgin olive oil
4 cloves garlic, chopped
1 tablespoon fresh rosemary, chopped
2 pints cherry tomatoes, stems removed and cleaned
splash of your favorite fruit vinegar
salt and pepper
1 cup ricotta salata, shaved with a vegetable peeler
1/4 cup flat leaf parsley, chopped

In a large skillet, heat the olive oil. Add garlic and rosemary and saute for 2 minutes. Add tomatoes and move around with a wooden spoon for about 5 minutes or until tomato skins begin to burst. Turn heat off and splash tomatoes with a little vinegar and salt and pepper to taste.

When serving top each portion of tomatoes with a little ricotta salata and parsley. Great warm or room temperature!

flavor, flavor, flavor!

# Salads with Protein

**Butter Lettuce, Smoked Trout, Grapefruit with Greek Yogurt Dressing**

**Bombay Chicken Salad**

**Jenny's Favorite Egg Salad**

**Thai Style Flank Steak Salad over Butter Lettuce with Pineapple–Jalapeño Dressing & Chili Peanuts**

**Cafe Jonah's Olive Oil Poached Tuna Salad**

**Garlic Marinated Chicken Paillards on a Bed of Fresh Herb Salad & Goat Cheese**

**Cafe Jonah's Greek Yogurt Chicken Salad**

**Jenny's Shrimp Salad with Greek Yogurt Dressing**

**Super Health Salad with Smoked Salmon**

**Raspberry Marinated Turkey Cutlets on Mixed Greens with Goat Cheese & Pumpkin Seeds**

**Gotta Have a Healthy Cobb**

**Spicy Tofu Salad**

**Local Greens with Crispy Proscuitto, Goat Cheese & Poached Egg**

**Warm Chicken Liver & Shallot Salad on Butter Lettuce**

# Butter Lettuce, Smoked Trout & Grapefruit Salad
## with Greek Yogurt Dressing

**SERVES: 6**

3 heads butter lettuce, leaves separated but kept whole
2 pink grapefruit, peeled, segments removed from membranes
1 pound smoked trout, flaked
8 ounces Greek yogurt
8 ounces buttermilk
2 tablespoons chopped chives
2 tablespoons fresh lemon juice
salt and pepper

In a large bowl, gently toss butter lettuce, grapefruit, and trout. In a separate bowl, mix yogurt, buttermilk, chives, lemon juice, salt and pepper to taste. Dress salad to your liking and toss gently.

With a very sharp knife, slice off top and bottom of fruit with a knife so grapefruit won't roll. Next cut off the outer peel around fruit until you have a naked grapefruit. Insert your blade between the flesh of one section and its outer membrane and cut carefully to the core of the fruit until blade hits the relatively hard center. Guide blade down both sides of sections as close as possible to membranes and gently pull them away. When all sections are removed, squeeze membranes to capture remaining juices.

it's best to
hand-toss a delicate
salad like this!

# Bombay Chicken Salad

**SERVES: 4**

4 cups poached, diced chicken breasts (about 2-3 breast halves)
1/2 cup minced sweet yellow onion
1 tablespoon minced fresh cilantro
1 tablespoon minced fresh flat leaf parsley
1 cup golden raisins
2 cups red grapes, halved
1/4 cup thin sliced scallions
1 tablespoon curry powder
1 cup Greek yogurt
2 tablespoons fresh lemon juice
1 heaping tablespoon mango chutney (recommend Major Grey's or Silver Palate's, a favorite of America's Test Kitchen)
1/4 cup slivered almonds or cashews, toasted (optional)
salt and pepper

In a non-reactive bowl, toss chicken breast, onion, cilantro, parsley, raisins, grapes, and scallions.

In a small pan, toast curry powder until fragrant, stirring frequently for about 1 minute, being careful not to burn. In a second bowl, mix curry powder with yogurt, lemon juice, and chutney. Fold this mixture into the chicken. Add salt and pepper to taste, and almonds if desired.

*Toasting curry powder as well as many of our favorite spices releases and enhances flavor.*

# Jenny's Favorite Egg Salad

**SERVES: 4**

8 eggs, hardboiled
1 tablespoon Durkee's Famous Sauce
1 tablespoon real mayonnaise
2 teaspoons smooth Dijon mustard
1 tablespoon chopped fresh chives
salt and pepper

Place eggs in a pot of cold water, enough to cover eggs. Bring to a boil, lower heat, and simmer for 30 minutes. Remove from heat, drain and cool eggs in cold water. Peel eggs and crumble with hands (my favorite method) or dice small. Mix with other ingredients, salt and pepper to taste.

# Thai Style Flank Steak Salad
## over Butter Lettuce with
## Pineapple–Jalapeño Dressing & Chili Peanuts

**SERVES: 4 TO 6**

For the salad:
3 fingers ginger, peeled
3 cloves garlic, peeled
2 teaspoons red chili paste
6 ounces Mae Ploy Sweet Chili Sauce
1/4 cup fresh basil leaves
1/4 cup fresh mint leaves
1/2 cup soy or tamari sauce
1/4 cup dark sesame oil
2 pounds flank steak
1 head Bibb lettuce
1 tablespoon canola oil
2 cups dry roasted peanuts
1/4 teaspoon chili powder
juice of 1 lime
1/2 jalapeno, seeded and chopped
salt
1 each red, yellow, orange and
  green pepper, julienned

In food processor, puree ginger, garlic, chili paste, chili sauce, basil, mint, tamari. Slowly add sesame oil with machine running. Marinate flank steak in mixture for 6 hours to overnight.

Remove steak from marinade and grill or broil to desired doneness.

For the dressing:
1/2 fresh pineapple, peeled and cored
2 cloves garlic, peeled
1/4 cup fresh mint leaves
1 bunch cilantro, stems removed
4 ounces Mae Ploy Sweet Chili Sauce
1 tablespoon dark sesame oil
1 cup canola oil

In food processor, puree all ingredients except oils. Slowly add oils with machine running. Salt and pepper to taste.

For the chili peanuts:
Preheat oven to 350°. Toss peanuts in chili powder, lime and salt to taste and toast for 15 minutes, watching carefully to prevent burning.

Assemble salad:
Portion beds of Bibb lettuce on individual plates or platter. Layer with flank steak. Top with julienned peppers and chili peanuts. Drizzle on desired amount of dressing.

# Cafe Jonah's Olive Oil Poached Tuna Salad

**SERVES: 4 TO 6**

For the tuna:
4 cups extra virgin olive oil
3 sprigs thyme
1 lemon, sliced into rounds
2 pounds fresh tuna

For the salad:
1 tablespoon extra virgin olive oil
juice of 2 lemons
1/2 cup chopped fresh dill
1/4 cup capers, drained
5 Roma tomatoes, diced small
1/2 cup diced red onion (optional)

On stovetop in Dutch oven (or any large, deep, flat-bottomed pan), heat oil, thyme, and lemon slices to approximately 130°, or until oil begins to shimmer. Submerge tuna and gently poach for about 5 minutes, or until tuna is just cooked through. With tongs remove from pot and drain on paper towels. When cool, break tuna into small bits.

Add remaining salad ingredients to a bowl and gently toss together. Add tuna and toss again.

No need to buy sushi grade tuna here. Ask your fishmonger for tuna bits or a less expensive cut of tuna.

# Garlic Marinated Chicken Paillard
## on a Bed of Fresh Herb Salad
## & Goat Cheese

**SERVES: 4**

6 cloves garlic, minced
4 tablespoons extra virgin olive oil
salt and pepper
4 boneless, skinless chicken breasts, pounded to about 1/2 inch thick
3 small heads butter lettuce, torn into bite-size pieces
2 tablespoons chopped flat leaf parsley
2 tablespoons chopped fresh tarragon
1 tablespoon chopped fresh chives
2 tablespoons chopped fresh dill
2 tablespoons fresh lemon juice
1/4 cup extra virgin olive oil
4 ounces goat cheese

Mix together garlic, olive oil, salt and pepper; spread on chicken and marinate overnight.

In a non-reactive skillet, saute chicken breasts about 3 minutes on each side, making sure chicken is cooked through. Keep warm while preparing salad.

In a salad bowl, toss butter lettuce with all herbs. Drizzle salad with lemon juice, olive oil, salt and pepper to taste. Serve warm chicken breast on top of a generous portion of salad. Crumble a bit of goat cheese on each salad. This is also delicious with cold chicken.

A great piece of protein topping a fabulous salad is one of my favorite meals. Low carb and nutritious... you can't beat it!

# Cafe Jonah's Greek Yogurt Chicken Salad

**SERVES: 4 TO 6**

Incredibly easy and always a hit, this no mayo chicken salad is such a crowd pleaser that you may never go back to mayonnaise again. We use grilled chicken for maximum flavor.

4 cups cubed grilled or poached chicken breasts
1 cup finely chopped celery
1 cup finely chopped flat leaf parsley
1 1/2 tablespoons fresh lemon juice
2 cups 2% Greek yogurt
salt and pepper

Mix chicken with remaining ingredients; salt and pepper to taste.

# Jenny's Shrimp Salad
## with Greek Yogurt Dressing

**SERVES: 4**

1 pound fresh shrimp, deveined, tails removed
2 cups Greek yogurt
juice of one lemon
1 tablespoon chopped fresh dill
1 tablespoon chopped fresh basil
2 teaspoons chopped fresh tarragon
salt and pepper

Cook shrimp in a large pot of boiling water about three minutes or until you see a couple of shrimp floating to the top. Transfer immediately into an ice bath and when cool remove to dry on paper towels. In a bowl combine shrimp with yogurt, lemon juice, and herbs.

Salt and pepper to taste.

I am always looking for an alternative to mayonnaise so the discovery of Greek yogurt has been a revelation! I use it as a marinade, in dressings and as a baked potato topping. Even a die-hard shrimp salad fan won't miss the mayo in this healthy alternative.

# Super Health Salad
## with Smoked Salmon

**SERVES: 4 TO 6**

2 heads Belgian endive, trimmed and chopped
2 bunches Lacinato kale, center ribs removed and chopped
1 ruby red grapefruit, peeled and segmented, juice reserved
1 ripe avocado, pitted and chopped
8 ounces smoked salmon, chopped
3 tablespoons finely diced red onion
3 tablespoons extra virgin olive oil
salt and pepper

In a large salad bowl, gently toss endive, kale, grapefruit, avocado, salmon, and red onion together. Add grapefruit juice and olive oil while tossing. Salt and pepper to taste.

How about a delicious salad that will give you all the nutrients you need in one meal — protein, omega 3's, dark leafy greens and a few vitamins and minerals to boot? This is a great salad year round and if you don't like smoked salmon, use grilled or broiled fresh salmon.

# Raspberry Marinated Turkey Cutlets on Mixed Greens
## with Goat Cheese & Pumpkin Seeds

**SERVES: 4**

When I lived in L.A. a hundred years ago, I remember this dish from a tiny bistro I used to frequent on the Sunset Strip. Unusual and different and always a crowd pleaser!

4 turkey cutlets, pounded thin
1 cup plus 1/4 cup raspberry vinegar
1 tablespoon extra virgin olive oil, plus 1/2 cup
1 cup pumpkin seeds, toasted
4 handfuls mixed greens
4 ounces goat cheese
1 pint fresh raspberries
salt and pepper

Marinate turkey cutlets in 1 cup raspberry vinegar overnight. Heat a saute pan, add 1 tablespoon olive oil and saute cutlets about a 2 to 3 minutes on each side.

Toast pumpkin seeds in 350° oven for 15 minutes.

Divide salad greens onto four plates. Place hot turkey cutlets on top of greens. Sprinkle the goat cheese, raspberries, and toasted pumpkin seeds equally over the salads. Drizzle each salad with olive oil and raspberry vinegar. Salt and pepper to taste.

# Gotta Have A Healthy Cobb

**SERVES: 4**

4 slices cooked turkey bacon, chopped
1/2 head iceberg lettuce, shredded
1 bunch kale, stems removed, julienned
2 cups cubed grilled chicken
1 cup halved baby cherry tomatoes
1 avocado, cubed
2 scallions, chopped, white parts only
4 ounces goat cheese (the crumbly kind)

For the dressing:
2 tablespoons white wine vinegar
1 tablespoon lemon juice
1 tablespoon honey mustard
1 small garlic clove, minced

Whisk all ingredients together for dressing.

You have two options when composing your Cobb salad. You can use a long platter and line up all ingredients side by side to make a beautiful presentation and then sprinkle scallions and dressing over the top, or you can throw all that deliciousness into a giant bowl and toss with the dressing.

Who doesn't love a great Cobb salad? What could be better than a giant bowl of meat and cheese slathered with great dressing? Most of us are trying to head in a healthier direction so I've come up with a version that is pretty close to the original with some tasty variations.

# Spicy Tofu Salad

**SERVES: 4**

I have grown to love tofu over the years. There are a zillion ways to flavor this vegetarian protein and I like mine with a little kick!

1 block extra firm tofu, drained and wrapped in a paper towel with a plate on top
1 tablespoon Mae Ploy Sweet Chili Sauce (in the Asian section of your market)
1 tablespoon peanut oil
1/4 cup hoisin sauce
2 teaspoons chili paste
1/4 cup rice vinegar
1 tablespoon sugar in the raw
1/4 cup scallions, sliced thin, whites only
2 cups, shredded napa cabbage
2 cups shredded green cabbage
2 cups shredded red cabbage
1 cup shredded carrots

Preheat oven to broil. Once tofu is drained, slice down the middle creating two cakes and then slice into strips about as wide as your finger. Drizzle both sides with the Mae Ploy and peanut oil and broil about 3 minutes on each side.

Remove from oven and set aside, or chill for 30 minutes if you like your tofu cold.

In a small bowl, combine hoisin, chili paste, rice vinegar, sugar, and scallions. In a larger bowl, combine all the cabbages and carrots. Toss with the dressing. Divide onto four plates and top with tofu.

# Local Greens with Crispy Prosciutto, Goat Cheese & Poached Egg

**SERVES: 4**

Local greens... Yes! It's not that difficult for most of you to find a nearby farmers' market and invest in some freshly picked lettuces. You'll never go back! Better yet, grow your own. I love poached eggs on just about everything. Use local, organic eggs if you can get them. As with the lettuces, the difference is memorable. The crispiness of the prosciutto works perfectly with the crumbly goat cheese and the egg. Yum!

1 cup vegetable oil
8 thin slices prosciutto
1/2 cup flour
4 small heads red leaf lettuce
1 cup goat cheese, crumbled
2 teaspoons white wine vinegar
4 organic eggs
1 tablespoon chives, chopped
1/2 cup Cafe Jonah's Fresh Lemon Dressing (page 100)
salt and pepper

Heat vegetable oil in a deep saute pan until it shimmers. Dredge prosciutto in flour, shaking off excess. Fry quickly in oil until each piece is crispy. Remove and drain on paper towels.

Prepare salad by portioning lettuces on four plates. Divide goat cheese evenly on top of lettuces. Crumble pieces of prosciutto over all.

In a saucepan add 2 inches of water and the vinegar, bring to a boil, and reduce to a simmer. Break each egg individually onto a small plate and carefully slide from plate into the simmering water. Cook 3 minutes, one egg at a time, removing each gently with a slotted spoon, and letting excess water drain. Slide an egg on top of each salad. Sprinkle with chives and drizzle on dressing. Salt and pepper each salad.

# Warm Chicken Liver & Shallot Salad
## on Butter Lettuce

**SERVES: 4**

2 tablespoons extra virgin olive oil
1 pound chicken livers, patted dry
salt and pepper
2 shallots, sliced in thin rounds
1 sprig thyme
1/2 cup Marsala wine
2 tablespoons good balsamic vinegar, plus more for finishing
1 cup chicken broth
2 heads butter lettuce
1 small bunch radishes, thinly sliced into rounds

Heat saute pan, add olive oil and saute chicken livers about three minutes per side, adding salt and pepper to each side.

Remove chicken livers and cover to keep warm.

Add shallots to pan juices and soften two minutes.

Add vinegar, broth, and thyme and boil until liquid is reduced by half. Put chicken livers back into pan with liquid to reheat.

Arrange butter lettuce onto four plates. Divide chicken livers among the four plates. Sprinkle with radishes. Drizzle liquid over each salad and then drizzle balsamic vinegar over all.

Good Parisian bistros always have some version of a chicken liver salad. This is a quick, easy one to try at home. Bon appetit!

...to friends!

great food is for sharing...

# Grains

Jeweled Rice Salad

Super Healthy Red Quinoa with Sundried Cherries, Kale,
Edamame & Ginger Vinaigrette

Jenny's Favorite Wheatberry Salad

Fall Wheatberry Salad with Fresh Apples, Pears,
Dried Dates & Toasted Pecans

Gluten Free Vegetarian Pasta with Marinated Tomato Salad

Mediterranean Kamut Salad

# Jeweled Rice Salad

**SERVES: 4 TO 6**

2 cups rice, cooked
2 cups seedless green grapes, halved
1 cup dried cranberries
1 cup toasted pistachios, or any favorite nut (optional)
1/2 cup sliced scallions
1/2 cup chopped basil
1 bunch cilantro, lower portion stems removed
1 medium shallot, peeled and rough chopped
2 cloves garlic
1/4 cup red wine vinegar
3/4 cup extra virgin olive oil
salt and pepper

In a large bowl, toss together rice, grapes, cranberries, nuts, scallions, and basil.

For the dressing:
Combine cilantro, shallot, garlic, and vinegar in bowl and stir to combine. Whisk in olive oil slowly until all is emulsified. Salt and pepper to taste. Add desired amount to salad and combine, tasting again for seasonings.

# Super Healthy Red Quinoa
## with Sundried Cherries, Kale, Edamame & Ginger Vinaigrette

**SERVES: 6**

For the vinaigrette:
1/4 cup rice vinegar
4 tablespoons cherry or apricot jam
1 tablespoon peeled, chopped fresh ginger
1/2 medium shallot, peeled and chopped
1/2 cup extra virgin olive oil
salt and pepper

Put vinegar, jam, ginger, and shallot in a blender and whirl, slowly adding oil. Salt and pepper to taste.

For the salad:
2 cups red quinoa
2 cups Lacinato kale, ribs removed from leaves, julienned
1/2 cup chopped scallions
1 cup shelled, cooked edamame
1 cup dried cherries
1 cup toasted slivered almonds

Bring 4 cups water and quinoa to a boil in a large pot. Cover, reduce heat to low and simmer for about 15 minutes. Quinoa should be firm, but cooked through. Drain and set aside to cool.

In a large bowl, combine quinoa, kale, scallions, edamame, cherries, and almonds. Slowly add dressing and toss until well mixed.

# Jenny's Favorite Wheatberry Salad

**SERVES: 6 TO 8**

I love wheatberries! They are a healthy, nutty, tasty grain, and so versatile. Toasting wheatberries gives them an extra nutty flavor boost.

2 cups hard red wheatberries
1 red pepper, diced small
1 yellow pepper, diced small
1 green pepper, diced small
1/2 red onion, diced small
8 ounces feta
juice of 1 large lemon
1/4 cup extra virgin olive oil
1/2 cup pitted, chopped kalamata olives
salt and pepper

In a dry, hot skillet, toast wheatberries for 3 to 4 minutes. In a large saucepan, bring 8 cups water and wheatberries to a boil. Lower heat and cook 45 minutes to 1 hour until soft, but still a little chewy. When done, drain in colander and put in bowl. Add remaining ingredients, toss, and taste for seasonings.

# Fall Wheatberry Salad
## with Fresh Apples, Pears, Dried Dates & Toasted Pecans

**SERVES: 8**

1 cup dried soft wheatberries (hard wheatberries should be soaked overnight)
1 crunchy, firm apple, diced small
1 red pear, diced small
1/4 cup dried, chopped dates
1 cup Mandarin oranges, drained
1/4 cup chopped, toasted pecans
1 bunch flat leaf parsley, stems off and chopped
3 tablespoons maple syrup
1/2 cup fresh orange juice
1/2 cup extra virgin olive oil
salt and pepper to taste
1/2 cup crumbled feta (optional)

Rinse wheatberries. Place 5 cups water and wheatberries in pot and bring to a boil. Lower heat and simmer 45 to 50 minutes until wheatberries are a firm, but chewy consistency. Drain water and place wheatberries in a mixing bowl. Add all ingredients and toss. Salt and pepper to taste.

# Gluten Free Vegetarian Pasta
## with Marinated Tomato Salad

**SERVES: 6 TO 8**

8 Roma tomatoes, chopped
4 cloves garlic, minced
2 tablespoons extra virgin olive oil
1 tablespoon red wine vinegar
salt and pepper
1 pound gluten free pasta
3 cups chopped buffalo mozzarella, bite-size pieces
1/2 cup chopped fresh basil
1 cup chopped arugula

In a small glass bowl, combine tomatoes, garlic, oil, and vinegar. Add salt and pepper and marinate overnight. Cook pasta according to directions. Drain and toss with marinated tomato mixture, mozzarella, basil, and arugula. Add more salt and pepper if needed.

Gluten free options have become more and more popular and I have become quite a fan of gluten free pasta. My favorite brand is Tinkyada, the closest I have found to the consistency of good, old fashioned pasta.

# Mediterranean Kamut Salad

**SERVES: 4**

Kamut is the Egyptian word for wheat. It has an appealing, nutty taste and people with gluten issues might find they can enjoy kamut without problems. This salad is good hot or cold served with a protein.

1 cup kamut berries
1/2 cup ricotta salata, crumbled
1/2 cup thinly sliced red onion
1/2 cup small dice European cucumber
1/4 cup small dice red or orange bell pepper
1/4 cup small dice yellow bell pepper
3 tablespoons chopped flat leaf parsley
1 tablespoon chopped mint leaves
4 tablespoons fresh lemon juice
2 tablespoons kalamata olives, pitted and chopped
1 garlic clove, minced
crushed red pepper flakes
salt

In a saucepan, pour enough water over kamut berries to cover them by 2 inches. Bring to a boil, lower heat, and simmer berries for 1 hour or until tender, then drain. Place kamut berries in a large mixing bowl, add all other ingredients and toss together, seasoning to taste.

# Dressings

Caesar Salad Dressing

Cafe Jonah's Fresh Lemon Dressing

Ginger Maple Dressing

Honey Mustard & Orange Dressing

Lemon Tahini Dressing

## Caesar Salad Dressing

2 garlic cloves
1 small tin anchovies
2 tablespoons Dijon mustard
1 cup freshly grated Parmesan
1/4 cup fresh lemon juice
1/4 cup red wine vinegar
1 tablespoon Worcestershire sauce
3 cups extra virgin olive oil
pepper to taste

Puree first 5 ingredients in food processor. Add Worcestershire, and red wine vinegar and pulse a few times. With machine running, add olive oil in slow stream.

**MAKES ABOUT 4 1/2 CUPS**

Note: You can use anchovy paste in place of whole anchovies if you prefer. Anchovies are very salty so you probably will not need additional salt. Just season to your personal taste.

## Cafe Jonah's Fresh Lemon Dressing

Everyone asks for this salad dressing and it is ridiculously easy to make. Here you go...enjoy!

1 shallot, peeled and chopped
1 bunch curly parsley, stems removed
1/4 cup fresh lemon juice
1 tablespoon sea salt
1 3/4 cup extra virgin olive oil
pepper to taste

In bowl of food processor, combine shallot, parsley, lemon juice, and salt. With motor running, add olive oil slowly. Add pepper to taste.

**MAKES ABOUT 2 CUPS**

Caesar dressing...
Yummy on kale!

## Ginger Maple Dressing

This is a fabulously versatile dressing. It's good on salads, great as a marinade for fish or chicken and a perfect match for tofu.

3 fingers ginger, peeled (about 3 inches)
1/4 cup apple cider vinegar
1/2 cup maple syrup
1 cup extra virgin olive oil
salt and pepper

In a blender, combine ginger, vinegar, and maple syrup. Slowly add olive oil with motor running until mixture is smooth. Salt and pepper to taste.

**MAKES ABOUT 1 3/4 CUPS**

## Honey Mustard & Orange Dressing

I love this dressing. Sometimes I marinate chicken or fish in it overnight. Delicious!

1/4 cup fresh orange juice
1/2 teaspoon grated orange zest
2 tablespoons rice wine vinegar
2 tablespoons honey mustard
1 teaspoon minced shallot
1 teaspoon salt
1/2 teaspoon pepper
1 cup extra virgin olive oil

Blend everything except olive oil together in blender. Slowly add oil with motor running.

**MAKES ABOUT 1 1/2 CUPS**

## Lemon Tahini Dressing

Tahini pairs well with asparagus, spinach, or any of your favorite grilled veggies.

1/4 cup fresh lemon juice
1 tablespoon honey
1 tablespoon soy sauce
2 tablespoons tahini
1/4 medium sweet onion, diced
2 tablespoons chopped parsley
1/2 teaspoon salt
1/2 teaspoon pepper
1/4 cup Greek yogurt
1/2 cup extra virgin olive oil

Put everything except yogurt and oil into a blender and blend until smooth.

Add yogurt and blend. With blender running, slowly add oil.

**MAKES ABOUT 1 CUP**

gratitude is a virtue
honorably cultivated at both
souper jenny & cafe jonah...

# Much more than a village.

If I expected my first cookbook was going to be challenging for my "fly by the seat of my pants" way of cooking, my second effort was even more so. I have never been a great recipe follower, and I always encourage the people I teach to cook more from the heart than from the page, so there are many people to thank for getting me here.

Hope Mirlis, the woman who held my hand through *Souper Jenny Cooks*, stuck by me through this book offering guidance and support as well as a kick in the pants when I needed one. Thank you "Hippity"!

Joel Silverman, our fabulous photographer, agreed to return and take the pictures for the second book. Thank you so much Joel for always being supportive, calm, organized, and for producing such gorgeous pictures. I am grateful for you.

Angela K Aquino, our designer, gets my vision 100% and has been able to put my heart on the pages of both cookbooks. I thank you Angela for assembling my recipes and pictures into beautiful stories.

Jeannette Dickey, our editor, really had her hands full on this project. Thank you Jeannette for your patience with my lack of computer intelligence and for guidance on content. You are a gem.

Jan and Chris Schroder of Schroder Media have helped me through the publishing process with both books, and I sincerely appreciate how painless you make the journey from creation to completion. Thank you!

A huge thank you goes to the staff at both Souper Jenny and Cafe Jonah. My team is incredible and they have allowed me to step back from the daily routine to work on new projects and grow. I could not do any of this without every single one of you, from dishwasher to chef, so THANK YOU!

As always, I want to thank my wonderful family members for encouraging my wackiness and desire to live my life out loud. I love what I do and the life I've created around me and I'm inspired by all of you.

*Jenny*

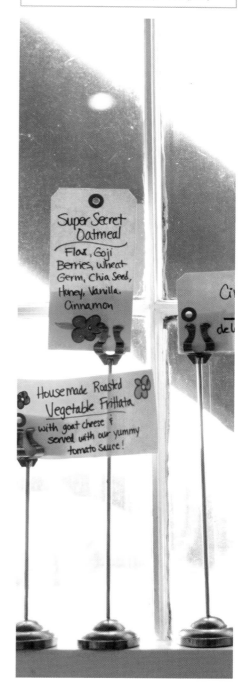

Jennifer Levison lives in Atlanta,
Georgia with her son Jonah and
two crazy cats. When she's not
traveling in search of her latest soup
concoctions, she performs in local
theatres and spends her time trying
to inspire everyone on the planet to take
better care of themselves and to be
more present in their daily lives.
Fortunately for her, there will never be
a shortage of people who need inspiration.

If you've got a story, request, comment
or question, please share it with
us at souperjennyatl.com!